Letters to You.

Published by ALMAZ AZMI

Copyright @ ALMAZ AZMI 2016

ALMAZ AZMI has asserted her right to be
identified as the author of this book.

First published in JULY 2016

ISBN 978-967-14336

Illustrations by ZAHIRA ZAHARI

Instagram: @almazspilledink

To the ones I love and the ones I will
learn to love in the future.

The thing about insecurities is that,

You forget what it is like to fall in love.

You no longer remember how to love yourself and see yourself worthy of such privilege.

But the funny thing about love is that,

It shows up in the unlikeliest of places;

Behind the most unexpected pair of kind eyes.

I don't know how long it'll last this time,

Because I am so accustomed to people leaving that I no longer root my heart and feelings to the ground.

But with you,

I cannot seem to stop myself from hoping

You would find a way in between

the spaces of my ribcage,

And anchor this wandering heart of mine.

Letters to You

You are the puzzle piece that I'm trying to fit into my life map.

I cannot seem to find the right combination of words to describe how terrified I feel when you break down my barriers like paper walls.

Yet it's exhilarating to feel like you're seeing me like no one has before.

I don't understand it,

This pull I have towards you.

I don't understand why you're choosing to stay when I've only got these tarnished pieces of me to offer you.

So I'm telling you the only way I can,

Through words I weave to sound like songs and love letters because I do not feel exposed when I write this to you.

Stay,

Please stay.

Even when I tell you to leave.

There is so much that I can give.

And I'm trying,

Trying so damn hard to unearth all the buried dreams I've forgotten about,

Because I'm sure one of them was to love someone like you.

This fragile collection of emotions I have,

Has always been prone to tearing at the seams,

Unraveling itself into a pool of madness.

My heart is chipped at the edges with a little less shine and a lot more burn marks.

You may wonder why I am telling you all of this.

Trust me,

It is not to be rid of you,

But to make you understand,

That I no longer know how to love right.

You came along
and taught me
that being broken,
Wasn't a weakness,
And having scars,
didn't mean that
we were irreparable.

I still remember you wrapping me in your arms and telling me that I felt like home.

I was silent then,

But if you were to press your ear against my chest,

You'd hear my bones shifting.

As every wall I ever built around me fell like a house of cards to make room for you.

Your lips remind me of
how it feels like
to crave for a kind of love
I've long left buried in the ground.

If I show you my pain,

Will you show me yours?

Mine goes down to the bone,

Long imprinted within my weathered veins.

Worry not about your own set of broken pieces, Love.

For I will fill the holes left by your past with pieces of me that were made to fit you.

I used to write my dreams on my palms and keep them closed tightly within my grasp in case I ever forget.
But you came along,
scattered kisses on my fingertips and made everything come true.

If I were to love you,

I'd do it with all of me.

I'd put my heart

and my soul

and the remnants of my tears

and every stained bone I had in my body into your open arms.

I'd give you everything there is to give because I do not know how to love in half measures.

Your love,

It was unconditional.

But mine was in pieces.

So I love you in fragments.

I loved you broken.

Give me your hand, Love.

I know that you're unfamiliar to tender touches,

But let me show you what it feels like

When two souls fit together so perfectly.

I love you enough to let my torn heart heal.

Staying broken was a choice.

It was a silent reminder to myself that even though this body of mine cannot shatter,

My ability to trust and love can.

Yet you have shown me the kind of passion that brought all my walls down to its knees.

So I wish you to know that,

I am yours,

Wholly and undeniably,

And it is enough for me to finally thread my heart back together,

Just to know what it feels like to fall into your arms and leave my fears exposed.

Letters to You

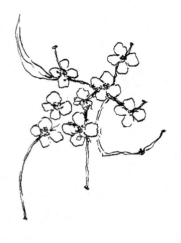

Lay here right next to me.

I've got a secret to tell you.

There is a new meaning of peace I have found,

And it is in the sound of your voice,

In the trace of your fingertips on my palms,

The unintentional smiles that pull at my lips when you kiss my forehead.

So if you ever doubt how happy you make me,

Just lay yourself right next to me, Love.

I will trace my feelings on to your skin.

You retuned all my splintered laughs and melded my cracked smiles back into shape.

It may not seem like much,

But it is enough,

Just enough for me to feel like I can learn to trust again.

I fell in love with the way you held my hand and the way your breath whispered across my skin as you told me that

it was okay to fall,
because our bodies may not have wings,
but our souls already knew how to fly.

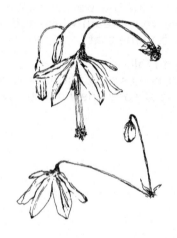

You are the kind of adventure my restless soul cannot resist.

Enchanting my heart with carefree laughs and crooked smiles that didn't just leave me breathless,

I forget the need to breathe entirely.

I seem to have lost my words around you.

For I have been too busy loving the mere presence of your body and soul right next to mine.

It's a different kind of belonging I feel when I am in your arms.

All I know is that I no longer feel like an aimless wanderer looking for the finish line,

And losing my words didn't feel like I was losing myself anymore.

Being with you has made me realize that,

That's all there is to it when it comes to falling in love.

You just have to trust your blind heart when it beats a little faster for another.

You remind me of what it feels like to crave for good morning kisses.

To sleep with a smile after hearing your voice at the end of every sunset.

To walk around in a daydream, because I held your hand and you pressed kisses inside my palm.

To look at the stars and not utter a single wish.

To simply be content,

Because you promised forever and I didn't have a sliver of doubt about it.

I could pry my chest open,

Discard all the incomplete pieces I've held on to for so long.

I'd make a space for you inside me,

To feel you breathe when I breathe and taste love the way you do.

Because,

You feel like you

You feel like me

You feel like us

And you feel like home.

So I'd give up all of the pain I've kept harboured within me,

Forsake all the bitter memories that has kept me from falling,

Just to make room for you.

Trust me,

I was made to love you and your imperfections.

Even when you tell me that you are too difficult to love,

Or when you warn me of your tumultuous mind.

I cannot give you the answer to all the questions you have about our future,

But I know that I was made to be Your light,

Your hope,

Your faith and

Your every dream,

Because our togetherness did not only feel right,

It felt true.

Let me make a home
underneath your skin
and burrow into your
dreams.
I'll loosen the
knots in your mind and
paint kisses on your
bones.
You do not have to hide
your imperfections around me,
For I too have holes
within my flesh and bones.

I want to be the place you bury your secrets in.

The one place you don't have to look over your shoulder and worry about your sins catching up to you.

I want to be the shelter you exhale in and allow your armour to slip off as your eyes drift shut.

There is so much of me that I want you to have,

And even when there is nothing left,

I will find more to give,

Just so you know that you have a safe place to breathe.

I'm not looking to be the one to banish all your sins,

For I can barely keep track of mine.

But our crooked paths and broken memories seem to align to form a map of constellations painted across the night sky.

And all of them seem to lead us into each other's arms.

Gently,

you pushed the slots of my broken pieces together.

Gently,

you reminded me that a man can love unconditionally.

You are a string of wishes I've made within this lifetime.

I'd like to believe that among those whispered dreams,

I must have done something right.

That somehow all the words I've spoken to the moon

And stars

And birthday candles

And wishing wells

Has led me to you.

When you pull me into your arms,

I am undone by your infinite capacity to hold me together.

Pressed skin to skin,

You stripped my soul bare

with the soft glide of your lips against my heart.

I am left breathless by how easy it is to love this togetherness we've built despite the chaos brewing underneath our veins.

I'll put my lips on yours.
Only because I am addicted
To the taste of love,
And you happen to be
my favourite flavour.

I've got a place for you inside me. Tucked away between my ribcage,

Nestled inside the space of my collarbone,

Pressed within the curve of my lips and a warm shelter inside my heart.

So if you're ever looking for somewhere to settle, Love,

I've got a place for you inside me.

I've always enjoyed the silence with you.

Because we didn't need words to explain how deeply we fell for each other.

It's hard to explain why I need you so much or why I feel so deeply for you.

For I am the same strong person I was before we met.

I may stumble sometimes, I'll have days when I don't feel beautiful and I'll have moments when I question myself.

But there is a difference between being strong on your own and being strong with someone by your side.

That is where my need for you comes from.

I have tasted loneliness; I have walked my own path of self-discovery.

But I have not begun to discover us.

So it may seem like I am weak for always wanting you to be by my side or for needing to hear your voice at the end of the day.

Because I am simply in love with having you near,

Knowing that I don't have loneliness as a companion anymore, I have you.

Please make space for me, my Darling.

I need to crawl into your open arms tonight and every other night that comes after.

You've become the only place where my soul knows how to settle.

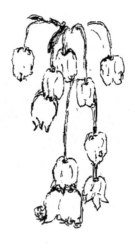

Tell me your biggest fears and I will hold you through it all.

I love the sight of moonlight when it shines through the open window to form a myriad of shadows and silhouettes across your naked back.

With the sheets tangled at our feet and the whispers of your breaths against the side of my neck,

I can't help but wonder if the universe looks down upon us and envies the kind of bond we found in each other.

Whisper your wishes to me.

I'll keep them safe.

The empty spaces within my chest have housed nothing but shadows and doubts for too long.

I need your dreams as light, Love.

I need your hope to breathe.

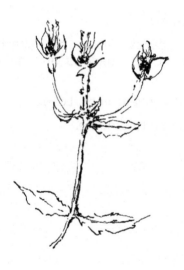

Don't ask me what love looks like.

I can neither picture it nor say it out in words.

But I can tell you what love feels like.

It's knowing that I have you to fall on when nothing else feels right.

I live for the
quiet moments we have
in each other's arms.
It felt as if time stood still.
Silencing the doubts
of our past and
Quieted our worries
for the future.
We were simply
allowed to exist.
To love
without consequences.

As we lay here,

Cradled in the aftermath of our love,

You run your fingertips down my spine and I taste your lips with mine.

You told me that I was your forever and I knew then that loving you was the easiest risk I ever took.

I love how our fingers slid into place.

Like you were coming home,

Like I had finally found my always.

You are like a silent storm brewing underneath
my fragile skin.

I find that I am simply in love

with the way you raise hurricanes

inside my once dormant heart,

and soothe my turbulent mind

with gentle rainfalls.

Lets fly to the edge of the universe,
Just so we can have forever
amidst the constellations.

Come and lay by my side, Love.

I'll colour the spaces of your empty heart with starlight and moonlight,

And scatter kisses on your fragile bones.

There will always be a place waiting for you in my arms.

I will never have it in me to say goodbye;

To walk away without looking back.

To pretend like I wasn't waiting for you to come home.

Because my heart is entirely yours,

Even if our lips become too tired to say the words anymore.

Being with you has led to all my scars unearthing itself from the hollow within my bones.

I no longer pick at my wounds and remind myself that time will eventually stop the bleeding.

Not when I have you to tear down this granite skin I've grown to cover the brokenness within me,

Not when I have you to scatter kisses on all the parts of me I have unloved.

Not when I have you to tell me that you see more in me than just a pair of sad eyes.

Don't promise me the moon,

I only want to lie on the sand and count stars with you,

Wrap our fingers together into knots that will keep us bound even when we are apart,

Stain our smiles with kisses pressed in between all the

'I miss yous'

and the

'I love yous'.

So don't promise me impossible things like the moon and infinity,

For I only want what is real with you.

You remind me of tranquil nights spent under the covers,

Running away from reality,

Creating dreams amidst the stars and silent midnights.

Play me one of your favourite songs and I will memorise it like a book of faith.

There may not be much that I have learned in this lifetime,

But I am willing to learn you.

To know anything and everything that makes you smile in your sleep,

Sing in the shower,

Dance in the rain and

Blow kisses to the clouds.

I may have been only a shell of a person all this while,

But I know now that I want to be filled with all things you.

Look closely, my Love,
You'll find that
My flesh and bones
Are meaningless
Without you
Holding them together.

You will always be that little piece of magic I carry with me wherever I go.

You sank your love so subtly into my skin,

Like mist creeping in at dawn across the horizon.

I've never been a morning person before this,

But you make me long for daybreak.

For I only see the likeness of your love when I see sunlight seeping through the lonely night sky.

I can feel the promise of forever with you.

I can see us walking with our hands linked and our smiles carefree even after the years have gone and eroded our skins.

For you have placed your heart in my open palms and I have fitted mine behind your ribcage.

I can never thank you enough

for being the voice of reason

I never knew I needed.

You taught me that forgiving

didn't mean that I had to forget,

It just meant that

I could look back

without feeling like

I left a piece of my soul behind.

It's hard for me to say the things you want to hear.

And maybe I'll never be able to put them in the right order to tell you how much you mean to me.

But I know that if you ever had a chance to look inside my heart,

You'd see your name etched across all four of its chambers.

I fear that you will grow weary
of my need for you.
There is no way to explain
How my insecurities drowns me
In self-doubt.
And I am so terrified
That one day,
You will have had enough.
Because in truth,
I will always need to hear your voice,
To hold your hands close,
To feel like I belong.

I do not think I can ever consider you to just be the other half of me.

No, you are simply infinite.

For you have taken my heart,

My body and

My soul.

And I, yours.

I understand madness now.

It's missing you even when you're a few steps ahead of me,

It's smiling at the idea of you smiling back at me,

It's the small laughs that escape my lips when I remember how I gave up on love until you walked in and made me believe in forever.

It's you.

The simple idea that you are everything I didn't think to dream of

and yet you are all the granted wishes I whispered at midnight.

I understand madness now,

because you take up every space inside my mind and I willingly embrace it.

With you,
It didn't feel like love,
It felt like forever.
And that's
what scares me most.

I want to grow old with you.

I want to sit by your side

And watch the leaves turn brown

And flowers bloom

And wilt

And bloom again.

We'd sip away time,

With cups of warm coffee nestled in our palms.

And our eyes would shine with the secret of knowing that we had lost track of love and found a path to forever instead.

Even at your worse,

You can ask me what perfection looks like and I will look at you,

Unblinkingly,

As I press a kiss to your lips and whisper,

'You, always you.'

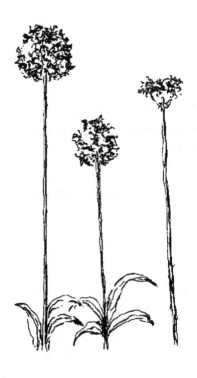

I've never fallen in love with anything or anyone quite as recklessly and irrevocably like I've fallen for you.

So tell me only when you're ready, Love. Because I know I am.

I love you.

CPSIA information can be obtained
at www.ICGtesting.com
Printed in the USA
BVOW06s0230211117
500205BV00005B/4/P